PROVERBS:

WISDOM
FOR THE
WAY

SCOTT WADE

Foreword by Bill Ulmet

PUBLISHED BY

MOMENTUM
—MINISTRIES—

www.momentumministries.org

DEDICATION

This book is dedicated in memory of
D. Eugene Simpson, my friend and mentor.
As Nazarene district superintendent of North
Carolina, he took a chance on me, giving me
my first pastoral opportunity. His wisdom and
grace have inspired me across my
forty years of ministry.

CONTENTS

Foreword.. ix

Acknowledgments xi

Introduction...................................... xiii

Did You Hear That?
Daily Reading: Proverbs 1 1

Promise vs. Principle
Daily Reading: Proverbs 2 3

The Generosity Principle
Daily Reading: Proverbs 3 5

Guard Your Heart
Daily Reading: Proverbs 4 7

More than Ever Before
Daily Reading: Proverbs 5 9

Get Out and Stay Out!
Daily Reading: Proverbs 6 11

Don't Fail to Plan!
Daily Reading: Proverbs 7 13

Age-Old Wisdom
Daily Reading: Proverbs 8 15

Mightier than the Rushing of Mighty Waters
Daily Reading: Proverbs 9 17

A Wedding Day Reminder
Daily Reading: Proverbs 10 19

Generous in Spirit and Deed
Daily Reading: Proverbs 11 21

Take My Medicine
Daily Reading: Proverbs 12 23

Starter Jacket
Daily Reading: Proverbs 13 25

Distant and Unfamiliar Territory
Daily Reading: Proverbs 14 27

Household Treasures
Daily Reading: Proverbs 15 29

Let Me Give That Some Thought
Daily Reading: Proverbs 16 31

What Makes You So Smart?
Daily Reading: Proverbs 17 33

A Church for Those Who Love the Church
Daily Reading: Proverbs 18 35

Be Careful What You Ask For
Daily Reading: Proverbs 19 37

Shine Your Light, O Lord!
Daily Reading: Proverbs 20 39

Of Course I'm Right
Daily Reading: Proverbs 21 41

Indebted and Enslaved
Daily Reading: Proverbs 22 43

Surrounded by Noise
Daily Reading: Proverbs 23 45

Rescue the Perishing
Daily Reading: Proverbs 24 47

Refiner's Fire
Daily Reading: Proverbs 25 51

Causeless Curses
Daily Reading: Proverbs 26 53

You Could Use a Little Perfume!
Daily Reading: Proverbs 27 55

Self-Evident
Daily Reading: Proverbs 28 57

Lane Reflectors
Daily Reading: Proverbs 29 59

Stop before It's Your Nose That's Bleeding!
Daily Reading: Proverbs 30 61

She's Little but Strong
Daily Reading: Proverbs 31 63

Conclusion 65

About the Author 67

FOREWORD

As I write this foreword for evangelist Scott Wade's book of devotions from Proverbs, I am reading another book he wrote: *The Climb: Stretch Yourself.* In that book (#4 of *The Climb* series), Scott writes, "But I have 'a building from God, a house not made with hands, eternal in the heavens' (2 Corinthians 5:1). Just as God knit me together in my mother's womb, he will fashion a new body for me." It's in the book. Take a look!

Now take a look at *Proverbs: Wisdom for the Way,* Scott's newest book. Here you will be challenged to read one chapter of Proverbs each day for thirty-one days. From each chapter Scott focuses on a verse or two with a significant message for the church and Christians today. For instance, he uses Proverbs 1:5 to tell us, "If you want to gain wisdom, then use your ears more than your mouth." Or in his chapter "Promise vs. Principle," from Proverbs 2, his wise counsel is "our hope can flourish even in the midst of delay." From "The Generosity Principle" (Proverbs 3) to "She's Little but Strong" (Proverbs 31), Scott will remind you of timeless principles found in the Word of God. Take a look!

I cannot add to what has already been written about Scott's character or even that of his wife. In forewords they have written, two Nazarene general superintendents, a college president, a lifelong educator, and Scott's own Nazarene district superintendent have already indicated this couple's humble, holy relationship with our God.

As a fellow evangelist, I also commend this book with confidence, for I have not only read Scott's books but I have also given them away to hundreds of people in my revival meetings. I believe they too, like you, will find his books challenging and encouraging—if they just take a look!

It's in the Book. Take a look and listen!

—Bill Ulmet
Tenured evangelist
Church of the Nazarene

ACKNOWLEDGMENTS

Lana Wade, my wife, has demonstrated unwavering love, faith, encouragement, and patience as I have quite honestly "failed" at retirement. Having her with me on the journey has provided a unique form of "wisdom for the way."

The rest of my family—my children and grandchildren—have also provided love, confidence, and joy as I worked on this and other ministry projects.

Several friends and family members provided devotional articles for this book: Aaron Beasley, Emily Beasley, Amy Berry, Sama Gilliland, Kenny McQuitty, John Wade, and Jenny Young. I appreciate their thoughtful contributions. They are recognized at the conclusion of the articles they provided.

Adam Toler of Dust Jacket Publishing has proven to be a valuable resource and encouraging guide to the process of publishing. That includes this work and several others as well. Thanks, Adam!

Once again Jonathan Wright has provided excellent editing services. Jonathan is a joy to work with—and somehow he makes me look good in the process!

Thanks to all the people who pray for and give financially to Momentum Ministries. You help provide the spiritual and financial resources we need to continue helping people attain, maintain, and regain spiritual momentum!

Finally, I want to thank the folks on the Momentum Ministries team. Whether board members or advisors, volunteers or "voices," you keep Momentum moving forward.

INTRODUCTION

As you journey through life, you probably find yourself searching for practical wisdom to guide your steps—whether it's how to handle relationships, make ethical decisions, or navigate everyday challenges. That's where the Book of Proverbs comes in, offering clear, timeless advice for the situations we face each day.

This book, *Proverbs: Wisdom for the Way,* is a collection of thirty-one daily devotions based on insights from the fourth book in the Climb series—*The Climb: Stretch Yourself.* My prayer is that each reflection will encourage you to deepen your trust in God and help you apply biblical wisdom to your everyday life. Whether you're looking to improve your relationships, make better decisions, or simply grow in your faith, there's something here for you.

As you work through these daily devotions, may you find that God's wisdom isn't just a concept from ancient times but is also still relevant and powerful in your life today. Each proverb has the potential to shape your heart, your mind, and your actions. So let's embark on this journey together, seeking to live with the wisdom that comes only from God.

DID YOU HEAR THAT?
DAILY READING: PROVERBS 1

SCRIPTURE FOCUS: Let the wise hear and increase in learning, and the one who understands obtain guidance (Proverbs 1:5).

DEVOTIONAL THOUGHT: Have you ever been around anybody who thought that there was nothing left for him or her to learn? Have you found yourself thinking, *I wish he would listen,* or *If only she would try to understand*? If so, then you can appreciate Proverbs 1, our chapter for today. The opening part of this book is a call for people to listen and learn.

As you read these proverbs, remember that they are not written to be understood as X + Y = Z, that if you do X and Y, you are guaranteed to get Z. Wisdom is not math. Your choices are not the only ones that impact you. God gives each one of us freedom, but we experience the tapestry of life based on where we are on the fabric—who is around us and what these people are doing. So instead of reading Proverbs as "Promises," read it as "Principles." Your life will be better when you observe its wisdom and worse if you ignore it.

Let the wise hear and increase in learning. True wisdom recognizes that knowledge is constantly one step ahead of its pursuer.

Two things are at work here: the wise do not know it all, and it takes a certain amount of wisdom just to listen. If you want to gain wisdom, then use your ears more than your mouth. We need always to read, always to seek new things from God, always to listen to those around us.

Let . . . the one who understands obtain guidance. If we think we know everything already, we won't accept guidance from others. But when we understand that we may simply lack knowledge, then we will be willing to listen to others and may even be convinced to change direction!

PRAYER: Thank you, Lord, for the revealed will of your Word, the still, small voice of your Spirit, and the combined wisdom of your people. Help me to hear and increase in learning, understanding, and guidance. Amen.

REFLECT: How has God's guidance through his Word impacted a recent decision in your life?

In what areas of your life do you need to trust God's timing and seek his will more?

PROMISE VS. PRINCIPLE
DAILY READING: PROVERBS 2

SCRIPTURE FOCUS: For the upright will inhabit the land, and those with integrity will remain in it, but the wicked will be cut off from the land, and the treacherous will be rooted out of it (Proverbs 2:21–22).

DEVOTIONAL THOUGHT: Proverbs 2:21–22 demonstrates that the Proverbs should be read as principles, not promises. Reading these verses as promises, we have trouble reconciling them with reality—not just our own reality but also the reality encountered on other pages of the Bible.

The problem with reading these as promises is twofold: (1) What is the timeframe, and (2) to whom is the promise made?

Proverbs 2 was written at a time when the nation of Israel was at its zenith. Solomon was king, the economy was good, and the outlook was bright. Later history and even current events reveal that geographical Israel has not remained the exclusive domain of upright people. It has not even remained the uninterrupted home of the Israelites! There have been times throughout history when the people of Israel were scattered and when occupying people lived in the historical land of Israel. Reading these verses as promises presents us with some difficulties. That brings us to the second question—If these verses are promises, then were they made to someone else besides the people who experienced occupation and exile?

Perhaps they didn't apply to those generations when Israel was in exile. But if we go there, then in effect we lose the power of a promise, for we can't say who is its recipient. There is no hope contained in a vague promise.

If, however, we view these verses as principles, then our hope can flourish even in the midst of delay, defeat, and yes, even in death. The principle around which I will build my life is that of being upright and having integrity. When I do that, I can know that my life will tend toward blessing and security—no matter what the outside forces and conditions may be.

PRAYER: Thank you, Lord, for both the promises and principles of your Word. Help me to claim what is a promise and to live by the principles—and to understand the difference—so that my faith may flourish. Amen.

REFLECT: In what ways do you find yourself focusing on immediate results rather than trusting in long-term blessings that come from living uprightly?

Consider how your actions and decisions can align with this principle despite life's uncertainties.

THE GENEROSITY PRINCIPLE
DAILY READING: PROVERBS 3

SCRIPTURE FOCUS: Honor the Lord with your wealth and with the firstfruits of all your produce; then your barns will be filled with plenty, and your vats will be bursting with wine (Proverbs 3:9–10).

DEVOTIONAL THOUGHT: I have a dear friend who loves God and tithes faithfully. Yet she often experiences financial difficulties. How do I explain these verses to her, whose barns are *not* filled with plenty and whose vats are *not* bursting with wine? I simply point her to the blessings of God in small ways and remind her how God has enriched her soul with plenty. I also can tell her that circumstances also determine what and how God will bless. Let me illustrate.

There is another place in the Bible that we can go to and read a promise concerning tithing:

> *Bring the full tithe into the storehouse. . .*
> *[Test me and see if] I will not open the windows*
> *of heaven for you and pour down for you a bless-*
> *ing until there is no more need. I will rebuke the*

devourer for you, so that it will not destroy the
fruits of your soil.
(Malachi 3:10–11)

In these verses we see that there are practical factors to what God can bless. He said he would rebuke the devourer so that their fruit would not be destroyed. That assumes that fields were being planted and worked! It further assumes that they were producing due to proper conditions. A dry season will have an impact on the crops of a God-worshiper too. But God will still bless. God will still make a way.

Whether principle or promise, a good life habit is to be a faithful tither. Good stewards, pleasing to God, must not only have the willingness to give but must also actually give! They must "honor the Lord with [their] wealth and with the first-fruits of all [their] produce; then [their] barns will be filled with plenty."

PRAYER: Lord, I thank you for the principle of generosity. Your generosity toward me enables me to be generous to you in giving tithes and offerings. My generosity opens the floodgates of heaven for further blessings from your hand. Amen.

REFLECT: How can you honor the Lord with your resources—even when it doesn't lead to immediate financial gain?

How has giving generously—whether it be through tithes, offerings, or other acts of generosity—impacted your spiritual health?

GUARD YOUR HEART
DAILY READING: PROVERBS 4

SCRIPTURE FOCUS: Above all else, guard your heart, for everything you do flows from it (Proverbs 4:23 NIV).

DEVOTIONAL THOUGHT: Since everything we do, all that we seek flows from our hearts, wisdom would tell us to guard our hearts carefully. But how are we to do that? Here are some ideas from Scripture:

Maintain thankfulness and praise to God in your heart. "I will give thanks to the Lord with my whole heart; I will recount all of your wonderful deeds" (Psalm 9:1).

Keep your heart focused on God. "For where your treasure is, there your heart will be also. . . . No one can serve two masters, for either he will hate the one and love the other, or he will be devoted to the one and despise the other. You cannot serve God and money" (Matthew 6:21, 24).

Trust in God with all your heart. "Trust in the Lord with all your heart, and do not lean on your own understanding. In all your ways acknowledge him, and he will make straight your paths" (Proverbs 3:5–6).

Ask God to purify your heart. "I will give you a new heart, and a new spirit I will put within you. And I will remove the heart of stone from your flesh and give you a heart of flesh" (Ezekiel 36:26).

Maintain a forgiven and forgiving heart. "So also my heavenly Father will do to every one of you, if you do not forgive your brother from your heart" (Matthew 18:35).

Keep your heart humble before God. "Because your heart was tender and you humbled yourself before God when you heard his words against this place and its inhabitants, and you have humbled yourself before me and have torn your clothes and wept before me, I also have heard you, declares the Lord" (2 Chronicles 34:27).

Guard your heart!

PRAYER: Lord, purify my heart! Then help me to guard it against unholy thoughts and attitudes, that my words and actions may be pleasing to you. Amen.

REFLECT: Consider the six ways to guard your heart outlined in the devotional (thankfulness, focus, trust, purity, forgiveness, and humility). Which one do you feel needs the most attention in your life right now?

What practical steps can you take this week to better guard your heart in that area and allow your actions to flow from a place of spiritual health?

MORE THAN EVER BEFORE
DAILY READING: PROVERBS 5

SCRIPTURE FOCUS: Keep your way far from her, and do not go near the door of her house, lest you give your honor to others and your years to the merciless (Proverbs 5:8–9).

DEVOTIONAL THOUGHT: King Solomon, a known womanizer whose appetite for women led him away from his firm devotion to God, wrote Proverbs 5 for his son. Speaking from firsthand experience, he knew how an undisciplined sex drive could bring great heartache. He wanted to spare his son from the same pain he had to go through.

Sin destroys lives! Sexual sins destroy families. I know of many people who have traded the joys of parenting, grandparenting, and financial security for yielding to the temptation of sexual sin. That's why Solomon told his son to keep far away from sexual sin. Don't even go near its door. What does that look like for today's generation?

- Pornography is often the first area of temptation today. We must build safeguards around our online habits. Become accountable to someone else. Give your spouse (or another person you trust) full access to your computer and phone. And when the pop-ups pop up, click out!

- Online relationships have ruined more than their fair share of marriages. Never have secrets. Don't even begin conversations with someone who might end up being a temptation.

- Flirtatious behavior must be avoided like deadly viruses. Don't even play around.

- Take care to avoid the very appearance of evil. Even innocently putting yourself alone with a member of the opposite sex is a danger to avoid!

Things haven't changed in three thousand years. The destruction caused by sexual sin is still just as costly. Strong warnings to avoid it are needed for our generation more than ever before!

PRAYER: Lord, confusion and lies abound when it comes to sexual sins. Help me to know the truth that is in your Word, and may that truth set me free from the sin and destruction of immoral behavior. Amen.

REFLECT: Solomon warns against going near the "door of temptation." What doors in your life may be opening you to potential sin or temptation?

How can you take proactive steps today to close those doors and put safeguards in place to protect your relationships and spiritual integrity?

GET OUT AND STAY OUT!
DAILY READING: PROVERBS 6

SCRIPTURE FOCUS: If you are snared in the words of your mouth, caught in the words of your mouth, then do this, my son, and save yourself, for you have come into the hand of your neighbor; go, hasten, and plead urgently with your neighbor. Give your eyes no sleep and your eyelids no slumber; save yourself like a gazelle from the hand of the hunter, like a bird from the hand of the fowler (Proverbs 6:2–5).

DEVOTIONAL THOUGHT: When it comes to debt—get out and stay out!

Solomon warned his son against going into debt, over-committing with "the words of your mouth." He pressed hard in this matter, telling him to take no rest until he resolved the matter. To me that is sound advice: Keep your debt as low as possible and get out of debt as fast as you can!

Spending tomorrow's money today is always a risky proposition. Here are some things that wisdom demands:

Do not keep a balance on your credit card! Use your credit card only to the amount that you can pay off monthly. Yes, you will have to wait for certain things, but having an older-style washing machine that is paid off certainly feels better than having a credit card balance that demands interest payments every month.

When you have to incur debt (only for your business or your house should be your goal), then pay it off as quickly as possible. It may be uncomfortable waiting an extra three years driving your old car around, but you will save thousands by not having interest payments. And never buy a car based on the payments! If you have to calculate the payments to see if you can afford it, then you can't afford it! Buy something cheaper. I know there are times when waiting on a car is not feasible, but when it is, wait!

If you buy something on ninety days same as cash, pay it off within the ninety days! If you can't afford to do that, then don't buy it.

So—get out and stay out!

PRAYER: Jesus, thank you for paying the debt that I owed for sin. Now help me to heed the admonishment of the Bible to "let no debt remain outstanding, except the continuing debt to love one another" (Romans 13:8 NIV). Amen.

REFLECT: What commitments or debts have you made that you need to resolve quickly? How can you apply Solomon's urgency in addressing your financial responsibilities today?

What steps can you take to avoid unnecessary debt in the future? Consider how waiting for what you can afford now might save you from financial burdens later.

Don't Fail to Plan!
Daily Reading: Proverbs 7

SCRIPTURE FOCUS: Keep my commandments and live; keep my teaching as the apple of your eye (Proverbs 7:2).

DEVOTIONAL THOUGHT: Chapter 7 of Proverbs is uncomfortable at best. The young man who is snared by sin doesn't seem to be seeking the sin that finds him. And therein lies the frightening truth that has been revealed from this proverb: we don't have to go out looking for sin; it will find us easily enough if we are not constantly on guard against it.

Consider two of the young man's characteristics that led him to his fall:

> *He went near temptation.* He knew where his path led, and the fact that he was walking that way under cover of darkness suggests that he may have had another motive in mind. I think we do the same thing at times—we try to get as close to sin as humanly possible without succumbing to the temptation. (I believe this is the whole idea behind pornography. Looking and not touching doesn't count as adultery in our culture.)

He stayed near temptation. While he didn't immediately follow this woman into her home, he stayed in her presence long enough to be convinced to go with her.

Satan, the father of lies, prowls the earth like a lion, looking to steal our joy and destroy our souls. Wisdom would dictate that we heed the advice of Proverbs 7:2: "Keep my commandments and live; keep my teaching as the apple of your eye." The young man in this proverb did not attempt to foresee the dangers and therefore avoid them. He had, in the words of Benjamin Franklin, failed to plan and was therefore planning to fail.

PRAYER: Lord, your Word is a path of life. Help me keep your teaching as the apple of my eye—to hide your Word in my heart—that I might not succumb to temptation. Amen.

REFLECT: In what areas of your life are you walking close to temptation? How can you plan better to avoid situations that might lead to sin?

What can you do today to keep God's teachings as "the apple of your eye"?

AGE-OLD WISDOM
DAILY READING: PROVERBS 8

SCRIPTURE FOCUS: The Lord possessed me at the beginning of his work, the first of his acts of old. Ages ago I was set up, at the first, before the beginning of the earth (Proverbs 8:22–23).

DEVOTIONAL THOUGHT: Proverbs 8, today's chapter, deals entirely with wisdom. In this chapter wisdom is personified, "speaking" in the first person. And she makes some pretty impressive claims about herself! The grandest is probably found in verses 22–23: Wisdom is as old as—yes, *older than*—the universe itself. When God set about creating the universe, he did so within the boundaries of something already established: his wisdom.

God's wisdom is evident in . . .

> *Physical laws.* The universe operates under an orderly set of laws that govern what things happen and how they happen. If A + B = C, then A + B will always equal C. Because of that, humanity has been able to make great strides in agriculture, in medicine, in health, and in technology.

Moral laws. These laws do not change because people choose to ignore them or replace them with "new and improved" moral principles. The best moral foundation is the one laid before the creation of the universe!

Spiritual laws. This kind of wisdom has been around since the beginning too. God made people spiritual beings. He created us to love us and for us to love him in return. He created us to know him and to be with him forever. Spiritually, our origin is in God and our created destiny is to be with him forever. God in his wisdom, however, has given us the moral ability and responsibility to choose our destiny. Choosing God is the wise course, but sadly, it is not the only course that people choose.

True wisdom is not something that is dependent upon the winds of culture or political correctness. It is rooted in the character and eternity of God.

PRAYER: Lord, eternal Father, creator of all things good and beautiful, help me today to embrace your wisdom, living within the blessings of your physical laws, moral laws, and spiritual laws. Amen.

REFLECT: In what areas of your life are you tempted to follow the changing winds of culture instead of God's established wisdom?

How can you align your life more with God's timeless wisdom?

Mightier than the Rushing of Mighty Waters
Daily Reading: Proverbs 9

SCRIPTURE FOCUS: The fear of the Lord is the beginning of wisdom, and the knowledge of the Holy One is insight (Proverbs 9:10).

DEVOTIONAL THOUGHT: What does it mean to fear the Lord? Is it a negative thing? Is it something we should do?

I can best understand the fear of the Lord by relating it to an experience I had while vacationing with my youngest daughter and her husband in Niagara Falls. I distinctly remember the feeling I had while walking along the Niagara River just above the falls. We had viewed the falls just before and had been overwhelmed by their beauty. We had seen 748,000 gallons of water falling over its edge every second. Now walking along the path above the falls, watching that water rush by just a few feet from me, I had an overwhelming sense that "If I fall in there, I'm a goner!" It was fear. But I wasn't afraid.

The fear of the Lord is like that. We are not afraid of God, but we fear him. We worship him in his beauty, in his power, in his holiness. But we approach him with respect and with reverence, knowing that we come to him on his terms, not our own. Just as we wouldn't think of swimming in the Niagara River just above the falls, so we wouldn't think of approaching God on our terms. We know that God loves us and that he sent his Son to die for us that we might come before him boldly. But we must come through the Son. We must come humbly before the throne of grace. When we do that, we have found the path of wisdom, and we can then have knowledge of the Holy One!

PRAYER: Lord, though you are mightier than the rushing of mighty waters, help me to fear you but not be afraid of you—to reverence you but not to hide from you. May I approach you with confidence because of your great love! Amen.

REFLECT: Proverbs 9:10 says, "The fear of the Lord is the beginning of wisdom." What are practical steps you can take to align yourself with God's wisdom in your daily life?

How does approaching God with reverence *and* confidence shape your decision-making and spiritual growth?

A WEDDING DAY REMINDER
DAILY READING: PROVERBS 10

SCRIPTURE FOCUS: A wise son makes a glad father, but a foolish son is a sorrow to his mother (Proverbs 10:1).

DEVOTIONAL THOUGHT: On the day I wrote this devotional article, my daughter was getting married. A few days later, my niece was to tie the knot. I thought it providential that twelve of the proverbs found in today's chapter have to do with speech. Wisdom in speech is essential in marriage and actually for all relationships!

If Solomon were writing these proverbs on speech today, you can be sure he would have thrown in writing, emailing, texting, tweeting, and whatever else we do to communicate. And it's not all just in the words we use. A shrug here and a rolling of the eyes there communicate as much or more than mere words. But even so, a smile here and an embrace there can do much good. Have you ever noticed how a heartfelt smile is emphasized by a twinkle in the eye? I love seeing people smile with their eyes.

There are twelve verses in Proverbs 10 about speaking. All of them include warnings against negative speech, while seven of them extol the virtues of positive speech. Solomon knew the human experience, that we all must fight against the tendency toward negativity in our communication. Solomon understood the damage a tongue could cause and focused against the misuse of it. To overcome the negative, we must intentionally focus on the positive.

So whether to newlyweds, already-weds, or never-weds, I offer this simple advice, something you probably already know, but it won't hurt you to hear again: Speak softly and gently to your spouse. Don't be "a foolish son [who] is a sorrow to his [family]." Let your spouse see that twinkling smile in your eyes daily. . . that same twinkle that you showed on your wedding day.

—John Wade

PRAYER: Thank you, Lord, for the gift of speech. Our words can bring healing and hope and happiness. But they also have the potential to bring sickness and sorrow and sadness. Help me this day to use my words to build up those around me. Amen.

REFLECT: Reflect on recent conversations and how your words have affected those around you. What changes could you make to ensure that your speech is building others up?

In what ways can your speech bring healing and joy to your spouse, family, or close friends? How can practicing restraint in speech improve these relationships? How can you bring balance to speaking out versus restraint?

GENEROUS IN SPIRIT AND DEED
DAILY READING: PROVERBS 11

SCRIPTURE FOCUS: One gives freely, yet grows all the richer; another withholds what he should give, and only suffers want. Whoever brings blessing will be enriched, and one who waters will himself be watered (Proverbs 11:24–25).

DEVOTIONAL THOUGHT: The wisdom that we find in Proverbs 11 stands out in stark contrast to what the world would tell us is wise. In a society that puts so much emphasis on wealth, material possessions, and financial "security," the idea that we will grow richer by giving freely to others is a foreign concept. After the federal and state governments have taken their share of our paychecks, maybe the natural human response is to feel that we have done enough. Once we get our hands on whatever is left, we feel entitled to every single penny. We feel compelled either to spend it quickly (before the feds think of another creative way to get the rest) or to squirrel it away in fear of the future.

But is this the attitude we should have as followers of Jesus? Consider the ultimate example of giving in Jesus Christ. If there was ever a person entitled to a blessing or a secure future, it was the righteous Son of God. But Jesus, "who, though he was in the form of God, did not count equality with God a thing to be grasped . . . emptied himself, by taking the form of a servant . . . [and] humbled himself by becoming obedient to the point of death, even death on a cross" (Philippians 2:6–8). He who gave of himself so freely was glorified through his death and resurrection, and the blessing that resulted was the single biggest game-changer in the history of mankind. It brings to mind the words from Psalm 112:9–"He has distributed freely; he has given to the poor; his righteousness endures forever; his horn is exalted in honor." May the same be said of us as we strive to become more and more like Jesus!

—Jenny Young

PRAYER: Lord Jesus, you laid aside all the comfort and privilege of your heavenly home to dwell with us in our world of darkness and misery. You gave all you had for our good. Help me to be like you, generous in spirit and in deed. Amen.

REFLECT: Jesus emptied himself for the sake of others. How can you model this kind of selfless generosity in your own life, both in spirit and in action?

How does the principle of growing richer through generosity challenge your view of giving? In what specific ways can you be more generous, trusting that God will bless you in return?

TAKE MY MEDICINE
DAILY READING: PROVERBS 12

SCRIPTURE FOCUS: Whoever loves discipline loves knowledge (Proverbs 12:1).

DEVOTIONAL THOUGHT: As I was reading this chapter, at first I thought I could ignore nine of the verses because they address the behavior of the "wicked," and I am not wicked. *Wicked* means "evil," "nasty," "vile," "detestable," and, well, you know what *wicked* is. And I am *not* wicked! A little selfish, perhaps, but certainly not wicked.

Then I slowed myself down to read just what those "wicked" folks are guilty of.

- Verse 2 mentions "wicked schemes" (NIV). Whoa—I have schemed to benefit myself at times.

- Verse 6 says the "wicked lie in wait for blood." I have occasionally wanted harm to come to people who have wronged me. Yikes.

- Verse 10 says that "the kindest acts of the wicked are cruel" (NIV). I have sometimes been cruel. Ugh.

- Verse 26 says, "The way of the wicked leads them astray." I have led my friends astray at various times. Uh-oh.

All these behaviors demonstrate my selfishness. If I replace the word *wicked* in these verses with the word *selfish,* then all of a sudden I can no longer ignore their significance. Here is how those changed verses get my attention:

- Verse 2: *Good people obtain favor from the Lord, but he condemns those who devise selfish schemes.*

- Verse 6: *The words of the selfish lie in wait for blood, but the speech of the upright rescues them.*

- Verse 10: *The . . . kindest acts of the selfish are cruel.*

- Verse 26: *The righteous choose their friends carefully, but the way of the selfish leads them astray.*

From time to time we all need the discipline of the Lord. This chapter was the perfect time for me to take my medicine!

—Sama Gilliland

PRAYER: God, help me to remember that selfishness is wicked. Help me to read your Word with open eyes and an open heart so that the words of 2 Timothy 3:16–17 are never diminished in my life: "All Scripture is God-breathed and is useful for teaching, rebuking, correcting and training in righteousness, so that [I] may be thoroughly equipped for every good work" (NIV). Amen.

REFLECT: When you consider the traits of selfishness compared to the behaviors of the wicked, do you see areas in which you might be acting selfishly?

How can you begin replacing selfish tendencies with selflessness in your daily interactions?

STARTER JACKET
DAILY READING: PROVERBS 13

SCRIPTURE FOCUS: Hope deferred makes the heart sick, but a desire fulfilled is a tree of life (Proverbs 13:12).

DEVOTIONAL THOUGHT: When I was in elementary school, everybody had Starter jackets of their favorite NFL teams. I was never one to be super into sports, but for some reason I loved the San Francisco 49ers. And man, did I really want one of those Starter 49ers jackets!

So for Christmas that year I begged and pleaded for my parents to buy me one. I knew the likelihood was slim because money was tight and the jackets were not cheap. When Christmas morning came, I knew for sure my jacket was under the tree. Wrapping paper flew off gift after gift, but my jacket didn't show up. When the last present was opened and I had no jacket, I thought all hope was gone. Then—out of nowhere it seemed—my mom brought out another present. She handed it to me and as I cracked the seal of the box, I saw my jacket. I came to appreciate and understand the value of that jacket so much more since my mom held off that short period of time.

I think it's much the same way with God. I think there are situations, hurts, or requests that we present to God and wait hopefully. However, as time lingers on with no answer or an answer we perhaps didn't want, our hearts begin to hurt. We begin to ask questions about "Why?" Or we plead for some kind of understanding. It's often in these periods of longing or when hope seems to have disappeared that we see God's love for us most. It's in this period of longing that we see God fulfill the scripture of Romans 8:28 (NIV): "We know that in all things God works for the good of those who love him."

God has a Starter jacket for you!

—Kenny McQuitty

PRAYER: Thank you, Lord God, that in all things you are working for my good. Even in the waiting you are working. I trust in you. Amen.

REFLECT: How do you respond when something you deeply desire is delayed or seems out of reach?

In what areas of your life do you feel your hope is "deferred"? How can you lean into the promise of Romans 8:28, trusting that God is working for your good, even in periods of waiting?

DISTANT AND
UNFAMILIAR TERRITORY
DAILY READING: PROVERBS 14

SCRIPTURE FOCUS: There is a way that seems right to a man, but its end is the way to death (Proverbs 14:12).

DEVOTIONAL THOUGHT: A few years ago I served as interim pastor at Memorial Church of the Nazarene in Orangeburg, South Carolina. The church is eighty-seven miles from my home on Johns Island, South Carolina. It is a "distant and unfamiliar territory." I was very dependent upon my GPS, especially as I drove home after the evening service. When it's dark everything looks different. It can be confusing.

One week I decided I didn't need my GPS. It was raining and hard to see. I didn't get lost, but I did go the wrong direction for a while! As I was driving around, a bit bewildered, seeking to get back on the right route . . . bang! I hit the median curb. Hard. So hard that it destroyed my tire. I didn't know the curb was there. I didn't know the danger ahead. I didn't even know that I had strayed out of my lane. I thought I was okay. I "limped" to a nearby parking lot and changed the tire.

We as believers are in a "distant and unfamiliar territory." This world is not our home. We were made for sunshine and light, not rain and darkness. On our own, it's easy to lose our way and think we're okay. The good news is that we have GPS to help us navigate—God gives the Word. His people are our traveling companions, and his Spirit is our guide.

As I said above, when it's dark everything looks different. Let's make sure that we use our GPS so we don't go the wrong way. Curbs are not fun to hit!

PRAYER: Father, I am confident that he who began a good work in me will be faithful to complete it. Help me to use my GPS along the way so that I can avoid the curbs and the destruction they cause. Amen.

REFLECT: How are you tempted to rely on your own understanding rather than seeking God's guidance?

How can you better use your "GPS" to avoid spiritual missteps or unseen dangers?

HOUSEHOLD TREASURES
DAILY READING: PROVERBS 15

SCRIPTURE FOCUS: In the house of the righteous there is much treasure (Proverbs 15:6).

DEVOTIONAL THOUGHT: "Retirement" life is different from the life of a pastor. I am just as busy as ever—writing books, preparing sermons, praying for and encouraging others—but I am home much, much more. And to my great delight, Lana is always (or most always) there. There is much treasure in my house!

"In the house of the righteous there is much treasure." It seems a bit presumptuous to apply this verse to myself. Then I remember that it is not my righteousness but Christ's of which I boast. He is my "righteousness and sanctification and redemption" (1 Corinthians 1:30). So this verse *does* apply to me!

Your treasure may look different from mine, but there is treasure in your house as well. Each of us has life and at least some measure of health. Each of us as believers has the joy of the Lord as our strength. We have peace with God through our Lord Jesus Christ, a peace that passes understanding. We have the family of God. We have the love of God poured into our hearts through the Holy Spirit. We have the promise of eternal life.

Yes, there is hardship and heartache in every house. Sorrow or sickness may be our experience at the moment. If so, remember that in all things God is working for your good. That is a treasure to hold tightly! Let's stop and thank God for the treasure that we do have; let's appreciate those in our lives whom we are given to love and to love us. If we will do that, then I believe the treasures in our houses will increase.

PRAYER: Father, thank you for the righteousness that is ours in Jesus Christ. We have been given a place in the family of God. And then, God, you have lavished your love upon us, filling our hearts and houses with treasure. Thank you! Amen.

REFLECT: What treasures do you recognize in your own household, both material and spiritual? How can you cultivate gratitude for the blessings God has placed in your life, even amid challenges?

How can you shift your focus from temporary, worldly treasures to the lasting treasures that come from Christ's righteousness?

LET ME GIVE THAT SOME THOUGHT
DAILY READING: PROVERBS 16

SCRIPTURE FOCUS: Whoever gives thought to the word will discover good, and blessed is he who trusts in the Lord (Proverbs 16:20).

DEVOTIONAL THOUGHT: Do you give thought to the Word? God has given us his book. It is a book of life for us. But we must read it and study it and apply it to our lives. We don't get the Word through osmosis. Giving thought to the Word requires the investment of time. In the book *Soul Feast* author Marjorie Thompson encourages us to approach the Word in an unhurried way, not to master it as much as to *be* mastered *by it!* Instead of just reading the Word, we have to be willing to allow the Word to "read" us.

An important facet of giving thought to the Word is to have a plan—the what, when, where, and how much. Reading through the Bible on a specific and disciplined schedule is important in order to give you exposure to "the full counsel of God." Otherwise our spiritual understanding will be deficient or lopsided.

Giving thought to the Word also involves interaction with others. Each of us needs to be challenged by what others see in

Scripture. We all read the Bible through the lenses of our own prejudices and experiences. Having the perspective of someone else will help you give careful thought to the Bible. Are you in a group who regularly discuss the Bible and apply it to life?

Another way to give thought to the Word is to apply it to yourself personally. Someone once wrote, "Read with a vulnerable heart. Expect to be blessed in the reading." That was the attitude of the Old Testament lad Samuel when he heard the voice of the Lord in the temple and said, "Speak, for your servant is listening" (1 Samuel 3:10 NIV).

PRAYER: Help me, O Lord, to give thought to your Word—to invest the necessary time, to seek the wisdom of others, and to apply to my own life what I discover. Amen.

REFLECT: How much intentional thought and reflection do you give to God's Word in your daily life?

What steps can you take to deepen your engagement with Scripture and allow it to "read" you rather than your just reading it?

WHAT MAKES YOU SO SMART?
DAILY READING: PROVERBS 17

SCRIPTURE FOCUS: Whoever restrains his words has knowledge, and he who has a cool spirit is a man of understanding (Proverbs 17:27).

DEVOTIONAL THOUGHT: Have you heard (or asked) the question "What makes you so smart?" It is usually said to a person who is sure he or she is right and wants everybody else to acknowledge it. That's what Solomon had in mind when he extolled those who restrain their words.

Restraining words is a lost art, isn't it? I'm not sure when it started—perhaps it was with radio or print media—but I know that by the time *Crossfire* aired on CNN in 1982, there was a move in the media to have people shouting down each other, crowding out each other's opinions. Then came FOX News and the twenty-four-hour news cycle with all the programs with competing voices. Something had to fill the air time! Daytime programming now has *The View*. The rise of the Internet saw many more outlets for unrestrained "speech." Now it's Facebook, Instagram, X, podcasts, and blogs . . . even email devotionals! Everybody has something to say, and it doesn't matter if it makes sense or not. Restraining words has become an archaic value.

With all the verbal competition going on, one wonders who is listening! It is only when we are silent that we can hear what another has to say. That's one reason restraining words brings wisdom. I've always heard it said that God gave us two ears but only one mouth so that we would listen more than we speak. Not a bad observation! Proverbs 17 ends with a fitting verse: "Even a fool who keeps silent is considered wise; when he closes his lips, he is deemed intelligent" (Proverbs 17:28). Another wise person said it like this: "Better to remain silent and be thought a fool than to speak out and remove all doubt" (Abraham Lincoln).

Are you restraining your words?

PRAYER: Lord, I know that "no human being can tame the tongue" (James 3:8), so I ask that you would empower me to restrain my words and to maintain a cool spirit. Through Jesus Christ I pray. Amen.

REFLECT: In what situations do you find it most difficult to restrain your words? How can practicing silence and listening more carefully help you gain wisdom and understanding?

How can you develop a "cool spirit" in moments of tension or disagreement?

A CHURCH FOR THOSE
WHO LOVE THE CHURCH
DAILY READING: PROVERBS 18

SCRIPTURE FOCUS: Whoever isolates himself seeks his own desire; he breaks out against all sound judgment (Proverbs 18:1).

DEVOTIONAL THOUGHT: I have often come across a sentiment seen on church signs and heard in mission statements of avant-garde groups, "We are a church for people who don't like church." *What?* That seems contradictory at best and self-destructive at worst. Are we to assume what they really mean is "We are a church for people who don't like any other church but ours"? That seems humble, doesn't it?

I once was in a discussion in which one of the participants said she believed the church was a man-made institution that more often than not got in the way of her spirituality. She believed that people were all good deep-down inside and that God was always inside her heart—she just had to find him. And she could do that on her own, thank you very much.

But is this what the Bible says? Is this the way Jesus feels about the church? Didn't he say he would build the church? Didn't he die to make the church holy? Isn't the church described as glorious, without spot or wrinkle?

Is the church perfect? Of course not! There are *people* in it! I once heard a pastor say, "If you find a perfect church, don't go there—you'll ruin it!"

The wolf gets its prey by separating the sheep from the safety of the flock. Satan is the master deceiver; he is the father of lies and knows our most vulnerable places. The only way to protect our hearts from this tragedy of believing a twisted version of the truth (also known as a *lie*) is to immerse ourselves in the Word, seeking earnestly the truth through prayer, and by being an active, worshiping part of the body of Christ through his church.

—Jenny Young and Scott Wade

PRAYER: Lord, you have said that you will build your church and that the gates of hell will not stand against it. Help me, O Lord, to immerse myself in the safety and love of your church. Though it is not perfect, it is being perfected. Though it is not heaven, it will help me to arrive there. Amen.

REFLECT: How can you embrace the church despite its imperfections and contribute to its growth and mission?

What role can you play in helping the church be a place of love, truth, and safety for others?

BE CAREFUL WHAT YOU ASK FOR
DAILY READING: PROVERBS 19

SCRIPTURE FOCUS: Desire without knowledge is not good, and whoever makes haste with his feet misses his way (Proverbs 19:2).

DEVOTIONAL THOUGHT: As I was sitting in a waiting room this past week, I heard the song "You Can't Always Get What You Want," by the Rolling Stones. It's kind of a strange song, but the chorus is really quite insightful, claiming that although you can't always get what you want, if you try, you sometimes find that you get what you *need.*

We do not always get what we want, do we? But often in retrospect we are so glad that we didn't get what we wanted! Perhaps we should sing, "We shouldn't always get what we want!" You've heard the saying "Be careful what you ask for—you might get it."

Have you ever made a snap decision based upon what you thought you wanted only to realize later that it was the wrong thing to do? I know that *I* have. When we desire something without knowledge, we may be desiring something that is very bad for us. "Knowledge" goes beyond knowledge of the desired object too. We must have knowledge of God's will. Sometimes a very good thing is not within God's will and having it would be a hindrance to our lives.

Often desire leads us to make hasty decisions. Sometimes we don't want to wait, for we know that more information will probably lead us away from what we want. In those situations we rush headlong into our error, blinded by two factors: desire and haste. Sales strategies are often designed around this very tendency: "Call today to get this deal!"

Are you making wise decisions? Are they based on God's knowledge? Do you wait for God's timing?

PRAYER: O Lord, grant me temperance in my desires and patience in my pursuits. Help me to make decisions based upon your Word and will and to allow you time to work things out. Amen.

REFLECT: In what areas of your life are you tempted to act hastily because of your desires?

How can you practice patience and allow God time to work out his will, trusting that he knows what you truly need?

SHINE YOUR LIGHT, O LORD!
DAILY READING: PROVERBS 20

SCRIPTURE FOCUS: The spirit of man is the lamp of the Lord, searching all his innermost parts (Proverbs 20:27).

DEVOTIONAL THOUGHT: One day when Jesus was talking with his disciples, he said, "Your eye is the lamp of your body. When your eye is healthy, your whole body is full of light, but when it is bad, your body is full of darkness" (Luke 11:34). This is what the writer of Proverbs was referring to when he wrote centuries before, "The spirit of man is the lamp of the Lord, searching all his innermost parts" (Proverbs 20:27). God speaks to us through the spirit within us—our consciences. Aren't you grateful for your conscience? God has given each one of us this inner light to reveal what is right and wrong. He searches our hearts and reveals to us our spiritual needs.

But we can dim our consciences—even snuff out the lamp of the Lord within us:

If we willingly disobey the Lord, Jesus warns us, our "body is full of darkness" (Matthew 6:23).

Rejecting truth also brings darkness: "Because they refused to love the truth. . . . Therefore God sends them a strong delusion, so that they may believe what is false, in order that all may be condemned who did not believe the truth but had pleasure in unrighteousness" (2 Thessalonians 2:10–12). Loving the wrong thing can snuff out the light within us!

John wrote that a lack of love will also cause spiritual darkness: "Whoever hates his brother is in the darkness and walks in the darkness, and does not know where he is going, because the darkness has blinded his eyes" (1 John 2:11).

God's Word is "a lamp to my feet and a light to my path" (Psalm 119:105). Praise the Lord! He is faithful to shine his truth into our lives! Are you letting it get through?

PRAYER: Thank you, Lord, for shining the light of your Word and your Spirit into my spirit. Search my innermost parts, O God, and give me strength to follow you out of the darkness into your marvelous light. Amen.

REFLECT: In what areas of your life are you at risk of walking in darkness by rejecting truth or harboring negative feelings?

How can you realign your heart to God's truth and let his Word be a consistent light on your path?

OF COURSE I'M RIGHT
DAILY READING: PROVERBS 21

SCRIPTURE FOCUS: Every way of a man is right in his own eyes, but the Lord weighs the heart. To do righteousness and justice is more acceptable to the Lord than sacrifice. . . . No wisdom, no understanding, no counsel can avail against the Lord (Proverbs 21:2–3, 30).

DEVOTIONAL THOUGHT: Do you think you're right? Of course you do! We all think we're right. If we didn't we would change our minds! Even in those instances in which we say, "I know this isn't right, but I'm going to do it anyway because . . ." we're saying, "This wouldn't be right for you, but in *my* present circumstances it is right." We justify ourselves. That's why it's so important to know what the Word of God says and subsequently to allow the Lord to weigh our hearts.

Often when we seek to justify ourselves, we substitute religious observances for righteousness. We "sacrifice"—give an offering, go to church, serve on a committee—instead of truly doing what we know to be right. We are in essence trying to atone for our misdeeds by religious behavior. The Lord is not interested in our outward acts of righteousness unless they are motivated by a true desire to be righteous and just.

At times we are able to fool others—even ourselves! through our religious behavior, but we cannot fool God. There is no justification that we can offer, no experts we can quote, no logic to which we can appeal that will avail against the truth. Our society is attempting to do this very thing as we seek to justify more and more deviant behavior. All the bluster, anger, and protests do not change the fact that God's Word abides forever.

Those searching for peace and freedom won't find it in shifting cultural mores. Only the truth will set us free.

PRAYER: Help me, O Lord, to be honest and true in the assessment of my heart and life. Then grant that I would be able to do what is right and just. Amen.

REFLECT: In what areas of your life do you tend to justify your actions, even when you know they may not align with God's will?

How can you allow God to "weigh your heart" and lead you toward righteousness rather than relying on self-justification?

INDEBTED AND ENSLAVED
DAILY READING: PROVERBS 22

SCRIPTURE FOCUS: The borrower is the slave of the lender (Proverbs 22:7).

DEVOTIONAL THOUGHT: It was 2015. Greece was being forced by the European Union into making significant changes to their national budget. The people of Greece didn't want to be told how to spend their money. They protested and rioted. The prime minister, who had been elected with promises of facing down the EU, did not want to accept the austerity measures.

I watched the news with bemusement. It really was amazing that a sovereign nation would find itself in the position of being forced—without any shots fired!—to do things that they didn't want to do. But what choice did they have? They were out of money. They found themselves enslaved because of their debt to the EU. Sadly, I realized that America is quickly moving that way as we drive up our national debt.

Indebtedness works that same way in our personal finances when our appetite for spending and consuming is so great that it drives us to borrow, borrow, borrow. Then we become enslaved to our creditors. We work day and night just to pay off our interest. Debt just piles up as we make our purchases with plans to pay for them later.

Jesus said, "Where your treasure is, there your heart will be also" (Matthew 6:21). When our treasure is entirely in the hands of lenders, our hearts are taken captive. We find ourselves pledging loyalty to these debt masters. Listen to the words of the wise—avoid debt at all costs!

PRAYER: Lord, help me to be wise in my use of money and in my acquisition of debt. Give me grace to get out of debt and to stay out. Help me to curb my appetite and quell my spending. May my treasure and my heart be fixed on you. Amen.

REFLECT: How does debt influence your personal freedom and peace of mind? What steps can you take to reduce debt in your life and avoid becoming "enslaved" to lenders?

How can you better align your financial decisions with Jesus's teaching that "where your treasure is, there your heart will be also"? What changes can you make to ensure that your treasure and your heart are focused on God rather than material possessions?

SURROUNDED BY NOISE
DAILY READING: PROVERBS 23

SCRIPTURE FOCUS: Apply your heart to instruction and your ear to words of knowledge (Proverbs 23:12).

DEVOTIONAL THOUGHT: In our culture it is becoming increasingly difficult to find knowledge. In fact, the "smarter" we become the less knowledge it seems we have. Technological advances have made all the answers an easy click away. Experts can save us a lot of time by telling us in their self-help books exactly how and what we should think. In reality, we are surrounded by a lot of noise. The noise distracts us from the true source of knowledge, which is exactly what our enemy wants. True knowledge can be found only in Christ, in whom are "hidden all the treasures of wisdom and knowledge" (Colossians 2:3).

In a world full of easy answers we are called to take the path of faith. How do we discern true knowledge? We cannot on our own but must rely on the Holy Spirit, as Paul reminds the church in Corinth. Those things that no eye has seen, no ear heard, no heart of man imagined, "these things God has revealed to us through the Spirit. For the Spirit searches everything, even the depths of God" (1 Corinthians 2:10). Paul also tells us that we can rely on the indwelling Spirit for discernment. "Now we have received not the spirit of the world, but the Spirit who is from God, that we might understand the things freely given us by God. And we impart this in words not taught by human wisdom but taught by the Spirit, interpreting spiritual truths to those who are spiritual" (1 Corinthians 2:12–13). Praise God for his provision. He gives us not only true knowledge through Christ but also an interpreter!

However, our hearts have to be in it, not just our minds! Are you applying your heart to the instruction of the Lord?

—Jenny Young

PRAYER: Thank you, Lord, that you are my teacher of new and wonderful truth and you also are my interpreter of what I learn from other sources. Help me to put my full heart into following your truth. Amen.

REFLECT: How do you ensure that the knowledge you seek comes from Christ and not from the "noise" of the world? What steps can you take to focus more on God's wisdom in your daily life?

Are you fully engaging both your heart and mind in seeking God's instruction? How can you do so?

RESCUE THE PERISHING
DAILY READING: PROVERBS 24

SCRIPTURE FOCUS: Rescue those who are being taken away to death; hold back those who are stumbling to the slaughter. If you say, "Behold, we did not know this," does not he who weighs the heart perceive it? Does not he who keeps watch over your soul know it, and will he not repay man according to his work? (Proverbs 24:11–12).

DEVOTIONAL THOUGHT: How involved are we in the rescue of the lost? Perhaps the question should be "How much do we love the lost?" One young teenager wrote this on her youth group Facebook page:

> John 3:16 is one of those verses that most of us could quote all day because it is used so often. I was really thinking about it the other day though. Sometimes when you hear something so often it just becomes a memorized statement. . . . In John 3:16 it says "For God so LOVED the world . . ." When I really think about that, it astonishes me. God loved the world that much. A place full of hate, evil, and

people that betray him. That didn't change his mind. In fact he did that not only for the people that love him in return, but for the people that have betrayed him. God wants us to show them his love through our love so that they may ask for forgiveness and turn their life to God. So that then they can show others compassion and love that know no compassion and love . . . just as "God so loved the world." (Katie Mounts)

I could not have said it better.

God loved the world too much to sit idly by and watch people sentence themselves to hell. So he did something about it. He sent a rescuer: Jesus Christ. Are we willing to be sent as was Jesus? Let us consider once again the words of that old hymn:

> *Rescue the perishing;*
> *Care for the dying;*
> *Snatch them in pity from sin and the grave.*
> *Weep o'er the erring one;*
> *Lift up the fallen;*
> *Tell them of Jesus, the Mighty to save.*
> *Rescue the perishing;*
> *Care for the dying.*
> *Jesus is merciful;*
> *Jesus will save.*

—Fanny Crosby

PRAYER: Lord, in the busy pace of my life I often lose sight of the fact that people are lost and dying—away from you. Spur my mind to remember their plight, O God, and help me to do my part to rescue the perishing! Amen.

REFLECT: How often do you think about the spiritual state of those around you? What can you do to demonstrate God's love and compassion toward those who are far from him?

In what ways can you be more actively involved in "rescuing the perishing" in your community or circle of influence? What small steps can you take to share the love of Jesus with those who may be stumbling toward destruction?

REFINER'S FIRE

DAILY READING: PROVERBS 25

SCRIPTURE FOCUS: Take away the dross from the silver, and the smith has material for a vessel (Proverbs 25:4).

DEVOTIONAL THOUGHT: An ancient refiner knew silver was pure if he could see his image reflected perfectly when he looked into the molten metal. It was only then that the purified material would be cooled into sheets or bars and the silversmith could hammer it into shape—to be the vessel he desired. Without the purifying process, the silver would crack and break. It could not withstand the repeated blows by the smith's hammer.

Think about the purity of your heart in light of the smith's (God's) purpose for you. How can you know his purpose for you? What was his purpose? Jesus himself stated that—

> "The Son of Man came not to be
> served but to serve, and to give his
> life as a ransom for many"
> (Matthew 20:28).

> "The Son of Man came to seek
> and to save the lost"
> (Luke 19:10).

Ask yourself, "Is the salvation of the lost my purpose? Is my heart purified for that purpose?"

What is the dross that might need to be removed in order to purify our hearts for Jesus's purpose? Three things come to mind:

- *Sin.* We must be done with sin—both actual sins and the sin nature. We cannot be effective vessels for God to use in the salvation story if our lives are controlled by sin.

- *Stuff.* The writer of Hebrews talks about laying aside "every weight, and sin which clings so closely" (Hebrews 12:1). In addition to doing away with sin, we must be careful not to become encumbered by the weights of this life: possessions, relationships, attitudes, fears, worldly values, the praise of people, and so on.

- *Self.* Your life is not your own. You have been bought at a price. Will you glorify God with your body?

PRAYER: "Purify my heart. Let me be as gold and precious silver. Purify my heart. . . . Refiner's fire! My heart's one desire is to be holy, set apart for You, Lord . . . ready to do your will." Amen. (From Brian Doerksen)

REFLECT: Are you ready to be molded by the "smith's hammer" for God's purpose? What impurities (sin, distractions, self-centeredness) may be hindering you from fully serving God's purpose?

How can you allow God's refining process to purify your heart and prepare you for his work?

Causeless Curses
Daily Reading: Proverbs 26

SCRIPTURE FOCUS: Like a sparrow in its flitting, like a swallow in its flying, a curse that is causeless does not alight (Proverbs 26:2).

DEVOTIONAL THOUGHT: The NIV wording of verse 2 ends with "an undeserved curse does not come to rest." A flitting and fluttering sparrow or swallow darts here and there without coming to rest. So also does a curse that is causeless. *Matthew Henry's Commentary* presents an interesting observation about this verse:

> The folly of passion. It makes men scatter causeless curses, wishing ill to others upon presumption that they are bad and have done ill, when either they mistake the person or misunderstand the fact, or they call evil good and good evil.

How often do we scatter "curses" or ill will to a perfect stranger? Think of the driver who pulls out in front of you on the highway or the lady who picks up the last item in the store that you were eyeing. How quickly we form unwarranted judgments about these people and even wish them ill in our moments of indignation! These causeless curses do not come to rest on the individuals to whom they were directed but rather inflict harm on ourselves, who utter them or think them in anger.

"Everyone should be quick to listen, slow to speak and slow to become angry" (James 1:19 NIV). Do you remember the story of David and Goliath? The giant did not want to listen to David. He was quick to become angry and quick to blare out curses upon the young shepherd boy. Let's not be like Goliath. Let's not finish face down in the dirt.

—Emily and Aaron Beasley

PRAYER: Lord, I confess that sometimes my patience wears thin and I harbor resentment—and even ill will—against someone who has offended me. Forgive me, Lord. Then help me to control not only my tongue but also my attitude, that I might not speak ill of my brothers or sisters, who are made in your image. Amen.

REFLECT: In what ways can you work on controlling not just your words but also your internal attitude toward people who frustrate or offend you?

How can you cultivate more grace and patience in those moments?

YOU COULD USE A LITTLE PERFUME!
DAILY READING: PROVERBS 27

SCRIPTURE FOCUS: Oil and perfume make the heart glad, and the sweetness of a friend comes from his earnest counsel (Proverbs 27:9).

DEVOTIONAL THOUGHT: All right, girls—oil and perfume do indeed make the heart glad! I'm sure the husbands can agree! In the wise words of French fashion designer Coco Chanel, "A woman who doesn't wear perfume has no future." Can I get an amen?

As a teenager I copied my sister's perfume choice every time she bought a new one, figuring that she was saving me a lot of time and effort to have to go pick one out myself! It got to the point at which she would hide what she bought so that I would stop trying to smell like her. Ahh—sister-copying at its finest! Anyway, the larger point of this is that my aromatic sister always had good counsel for me, and I appreciated that so much. And yes, I still copy her perfume choices.

Here's the challenge for you today: Are you a friend who brings that sweet fragrance to others? Do you prayerfully counsel your friends in need, or do you find that you are constantly requiring all the oil for yourself? I'm not talking about when you're going through a hard time but rather simply in day-to-day life: Are you giving to others to the best of your ability, covering them with your love and prayer, smothering them with your sweet scent?

My charge to you is going to be the same as that of the author of this chapter of Proverbs—to be a faithful and constant friend. We are, after all, "the aroma of Christ . . . a fragrance from life to life" (2 Corinthians 2:15–16). So turn your eyes to the cross—Jesus's model of unconditional love, consistency, and faithfulness. Then praise him for the sweetness of a true friend!

— Amy Berry

PRAYER: Thank you, Lord Jesus, that you call me your friend. Thank you that you are a friend who sticks closer than even a brother or sister. Help me to be the kind of friend to others that you are to me. Amen.

REFLECT: How can you be more intentional about being a "sweet fragrance" in the lives of those around you?

Are you constantly requiring encouragement and support from others, or are you also giving it back in return? What steps can you take to balance both receiving and giving friendship and care in your relationships?

SELF-EVIDENT
DAILY READING: PROVERBS 28

SCRIPTURE FOCUS: Evil men do not understand justice, but those who seek the Lord understand it completely (Proverbs 28:5).

DEVOTIONAL THOUGHT: In "The unanimous Declaration of the thirteen united States of America" are the celebrated words "We hold these truths to be self-evident." Those revolutionaries of the 1700s wrote about such things as equality and unalienable rights. Yet those truths were not so self-evident in the world of their day, and in today's world they are still greeted with skepticism.

In the days of ancient Israel there were also self-evident truths that found their way into the proverbs of King Solomon. These principles were greeted with skepticism then as well as today. Proverbs 28:5 contains four self-evident truths that fit in that category:

There are evil people in the world. The Bible explains that evil came into the perfect world when Adam and Eve rebelled against God (Genesis 3). As people continued rejecting God, they became increasingly evil (Genesis 6). Pop psychology may assert that no person is evil, that only deeds are, but the Bible is clear that people are evil and do evil to others.

Evil people do not understand justice. Evil is not universally accepted. Evil minds are clouded and deluded. What is evil is called good, and what is good is called evil.

There are "those who seek the Lord": This phrase is placed in juxtaposition to the phrase "evil men." It is self-evident that to escape the mastery of evil, one must turn to the Lord. Experience teaches us that this is a process as well as a crisis. There is a turning to, then a growing in, righteousness.

Those who seek the Lord "understand it completely." Understanding, like character, comes as a process. What begins as a morning light is destined to become the noonday sun.

Do you see these self-evident truths?

PRAYER: Help me, O Lord, to seek you and to understand justice. May I be kind and merciful and patient as you are. Amen.

REFLECT: Do you see the self-evident truth that evil exists and clouds people's understanding of justice?

How can you guard your heart and mind from the confusion between good and evil in today's world?

LANE REFLECTORS
DAILY READING: PROVERBS 29

SCRIPTURE FOCUS: Where there is no prophetic vision the people cast off restraint (Proverbs 29:18).

DEVOTIONAL THOUGHT: I remember when the department of highways first started installing reflectors to designate the lanes on highways, about forty-five years ago. White reflectors signified the right edge of the driving lane. Yellow reflectors indicated where the center lines were. I did not like them. I was a young—very young—driver, and I was distracted by the reflections. Over the years, however, I have come to be quite dependent on them.

One night I was traveling on I-275 on the north side of Cincinnati in a construction zone (when are you *not* in a construction zone on I-275?), and those orange and-white construction "barrels" were flying by my field of vision. The new lanes were marked with light temporary paint. The previous lane lines were still somewhat visible, however. Traffic was heavy, and I had lots of lights shining in my eyes. To top it off, it was raining and the trucks were throwing off sheets of mist. My windshield wipers were streaking with road grime and bug guts. Aargh! *Where are the lanes?* I sure did miss those lane reflectors!

Prophetic visions are like those lane reflectors. Without them, we easily lose track of what lane we're supposed to be in. A vision keeps us on track, moving in the right direction. The vision provided by the truth of the Bible clearly marks the road to heaven. Without that vision, people develop their own "truth" and will miss the right road.

How about you? Do you live by the moral vision of the Bible? Do you have a vision of your God-intended purpose? Are you engaged by the vision of Jesus, who said to "lift up your eyes, and see that the fields are white for harvest" (John 4:35)? Without a vision you will certainly *cast off restraint.*

PRAYER: Thank you, Lord, for the lane reflectors—the vision of truth—that you provide. Help me to move with resolute purpose on the road you have laid out for me. Give me a vision of Jesus, I pray! Amen.

REFLECT: How does having a clear vision from God help you stay on the right path in life?

Are there areas where you feel you lack vision or direction? If so, how can you seek clarity through prayer and Scripture?

STOP BEFORE IT'S YOUR NOSE THAT'S BLEEDING!
DAILY READING: PROVERBS 30

SCRIPTURE FOCUS: If you have been foolish, exalting yourself, or if you have been devising evil, put your hand on your mouth. For pressing milk produces curds, pressing the nose produces blood, and pressing anger produces strife (Proverbs 30:32–33).

DEVOTIONAL THOUGHT: You've been there. We all have. There's a disagreement. Emotions get involved. Voices are raised. Anger grows. A relationship is severed. Then comes regret. "Why did I press that issue?" Agur, the author of Proverbs 30, helps us understand:

- *If you have been foolish:* What is it to be foolish? It's lacking wisdom. In retrospect, how many times were your opinions, held tightly and cherished dearly, proven to be wrong? Many disagreements occur when people press an issue they think is right but is so very wrong!

- *Exalting yourself:* Prideful people delight in the destruction of others, in bringing others down to elevate themselves. Humble people, however, will lift others up, promoting goodwill in a relationship. It's hard for a proud person to admit he or she is wrong—and even harder not to press when he or she is right. Nobody wants to hear, "I told you so!"

- *Devising evil:* Harboring resentment for past wrongs, savoring sweet imaginations of revenge, the aggrieved person wishes ill will on his or her "foe." Getting even for past hurts overwhelms the person's senses, and when the opportunity presents itself, he or she presses the issue with caustic and hateful speech.

When we find ourselves at odds with another, what should we do? Looking at the causes helps us understand three things. First you need to seek wisdom and information. Try to understand the issue at hand, especially from the other's point of view. Then you need to humble yourself. Be willing to consider that maybe, just maybe, you're wrong and the other person is right. Apologize! Forgive from your heart—even if not asked for. And don't "lord it over" the one you have forgiven! Finally, do what Agur suggested: put your hand on your mouth. You might stop a nose bleed!

PRAYER: Lord Jesus, if anyone ever had the right to press an issue, you certainly did. Instead, you willingly took the penalty for my sin and forgave me from the cross. Help me to have the same mindset as you. Amen.

REFLECT: When you find yourself in conflict, how often do you press your point of view without truly considering the other person's perspective?

What can you do to stop and seek wisdom before escalating an argument? What steps can you take to put Agur's advice into action—"put your hand on your mouth"—to prevent unnecessary strife?

SHE'S LITTLE BUT STRONG
DAILY READING: PROVERBS 31

SCRIPTURE FOCUS: She dresses herself with strength and makes her arms strong (Proverbs 31:17).

DEVOTIONAL THOUGHT: In 1979 Lana and I moved into our first apartment. We moved from two places: her home in Barrackville, West Virginia, and my home in Montpelier, Ohio. Lana's dad and I loaded up Lana's belongings. My brother and sister-in-law, Al and Karen, loaded up my things and brought them to us. When we met, I asked how they got it all loaded. Karen said she had done it all herself.

"What?" I exclaimed. "I could barely lift those boxes! How did you do it?"

"I just picked them up!" My sister-in-law was only five feet tall and probably about 110 pounds—but she was strong!

Another strong woman is my daughter Amy. She is a little taller than my sister-in-law, maybe 5'2". But she weighs less. Amy has always surprised me with her physical strength. As a pastor's kid, she has moved a lot. During the last few moves she was the only kid left at home. When I needed someone on the other end of the couch or dresser, it was Amy I turned to. She has strong arms!

Physical strength is one thing, but the most important strength is spiritual. How does a person dress himself or herself with spiritual strength? Just as Karen and Amy worked their arms, we need to work our spiritual arms! We do that by serving the Lord, by searching the Scriptures, and by stepping out on faith. If we want to be strong in the Lord, another thing we must not neglect is found in Nehemiah 8:10—"The joy of the Lord is your strength." Strength comes with joy.

Just like my sister-in-law and my daughter, we don't have to be "big" to be strong. We can clothe ourselves with strength, the strength of the Lord.

PRAYER: Thank you, Lord, that though I am weak, yet I am strong, for your strength is perfected in me. Help me to work my spiritual arms and so grow in strength. Amen.

REFLECT: As you think about Nehemiah 8:10, "The joy of the Lord is your strength," how can you cultivate more joy in your daily walk with God, knowing that it contributes to your spiritual strength?

What practices or attitudes can help you experience this joy even in challenging times?

CONCLUSION

In this journey through Proverbs we have learned that there are principles to live by—guidelines for a life that is marked by righteousness, integrity, and faithfulness. Yet principles alone will not save us. Wisdom's highest form is not mere knowledge or prudence—it is a life fully surrendered to God's will. Solomon's own story bears witness to this truth. He who had known the extremes of both virtue and vice speaks from the depth of his experience, warning us not to chase after the wind. His life was a canvas upon which the lessons of Proverbs were lived out, but it was also a canvas stained by human weakness.

As King Solomon neared the end of his life, the sum of all his wisdom was distilled into a single, profound statement: "Now all has been heard; here is the conclusion of the matter: Fear God and keep his commandments, for this is the duty of all mankind" (Ecclesiastes 12:13 NIV). These words echo from a man who had walked the peaks of wild success and trudged through the valleys of grave sin, only to arrive at the proper conclusion—life at its core is about revering God and obeying his ways.

As with our own lives, Solomon's life took many turns. He experienced the depths of human frailty and failure despite the greatness of his kingdom and his own unparalleled wisdom. His final words in Ecclesiastes offer the reflections of a man who, after navigating through the highs and lows, came back to the foundation that had always been there—God.

Solomon's final analysis reveals that while wisdom, wealth, power, and even pleasure have their place, they are not ultimate. The beauty and practicality of living a wise and disciplined life are undisputed, but even wisdom itself is fleeting unless it is grounded in the fear of God. To fear God, as Solomon concluded, means to place him in his rightful position above all else and to recognize his sovereignty and goodness in our lives.

Thus, as we conclude this journey through Proverbs, we must remember that true wisdom leads us back to God. The instructions and insights of this book point us toward practical and righteous living, but the heart of the matter is always a posture of surrender before our creator: "Fear God and keep his commandments" (Proverbs 12:13). In doing so, we are fulfilling the very purpose for which we were made. What greater wisdom could we find on the way?

ABOUT THE AUTHOR

SCOTT WADE is the founder of Momentum Ministries, a nonprofit organization dedicated to helping individuals and churches grow in their faith. With a passion for writing, preaching, and encouraging others, Scott has authored several books, including the popular *The Climb Series*: *Start Here, Stay Focused, Stick with It, Stretch Yourself,* and *Stand Tall.* These books, alongside his Christmas devotionals, *Christmas with Luke* and *Christmas with Matthew,* have inspired many readers to deepen their relationship with God and apply biblical principles to their daily lives.

Scott's ministry includes not only writing but also hosting the podcast *Casual Conversations by Momentum Ministries*, preaching at revivals, and helping aspiring Christian authors publish their own books. He brings a wealth of experience from decades of pastoral leadership and now focuses on encouraging and empowering others to grow in their spiritual journeys.

You can find more about Scott and his ministry, along with his books, at *momentumministries.org*.